Galatea

Melanie Challenger is an award-winning writer of both poetry and prose. Her collaboration with Bosnian war diarist, Zlata Filipović, includes *Stolen Voices*, a book on young people in conflict which has been widely published and translated internationally. As a librettist, she adapted the Anne Frank diaries for British composer James Whitbourn's *Annelies*. She was the recipient of the 2005 Society of Author's Eric Gregory award for poetry.

Also by Melanie Challenger

Galatea

Melanie Challenger

SALT

CAMBRIDGE

PUBLISHED BY SALT PUBLISHING
PO Box 937, Great Wilbraham, Cambridge PDO CB1 5JX United Kingdom

© Melanie Challenger, 2006

Salt Publishing 2006

Printed and bound in the United States of America by Lightning Source

Typeset in Swift 9.5 / 13

ISBN-13 978 1 84471 290 8 paperback
ISBN-10 1 84471 290 7 paperback

SP

1 3 5 7 9 8 6 4 2

To my mother and father
and my sister, Tamsyn

Contents

Acknowledgements

Excerpt from 'Requiem' by Anna Akhmatova (1889–1966). Anna Akhmatova, *Selected Poems* translated by D.M. Thomas, Penguin Books (1988).

Excerpt from 'Santorini: Stopping the Leak' by James Merrill (1936–1995). James Merrill, *Selected Poems*, Alfred A. Knopf, inc. (2001).

Excerpt on page 16 taken from the introduction to *Beowulf* translated by Seamus Heaney (1939–). *Beowulf* by Seamus Heaney, Faber & Faber Ltd. (1999).

Excerpt page 19 from 'A Dialogue of Self and Soul' by W.B. Yeats (1865–1939). *A Collected Poems of W.B.Yeats*, Wordsworth Editions Ltd. (2000).

Quotes on pages 21—23 are adapted from the exchange of letters between Greek poet, Nikos Kazantzakis (1883–1957), and his wife, Galatea, translated by Ben Petre. The quote that runs from 'Magdalene . . .' to '. . . were ready to break' is an excerpt from *The Last Temptation of Christ* by Nikos Kazantzakis, translated by Peter A. Bien, Faber and Faber (1975). For further information, visit:

http://www.historical-museum.gr/kazantzakis/

'Everything visible is connected to the invisible' on page 24 is taken from the philosophy of Novalis (alias Friedrich von Hardenberg, 1772–1800). Novalis, *Philosophical Writings*, translated and edited by Margaret Mahony Stoljar, State University of New York Press (1997).

Excerpt on page 29 from 'And What's New?' by Miroslav Holub. This translation comes from *Selected Poems*, Miroslav Holub, translated by Ian Milner and George Theiner, Penguin Books (1967).

The quote on pages 35–36 that runs from 'Confronting is like . . .' to '. . . passing of ages has retreated into stone' is an excerpt from *The Master of Petersburg*, a novel by J.M.Coetzee (1940–). *The Master of Petersburg* by J.M.Coetzee, Vintage (1999).

Excerpt on page 37 from 'Medusa' by Hart Crane (1899–1932). *The Complete Poems of Hart Crane* by Hart Crane, W.W. Norton & Company (2001).

The quote on page 45 that runs from 'Perseus himself . . .' to 'great fear was quaking' are verses 228–37 from *Shield of Heracles* by Hesiod.

The quote on page 46 'Great thought is like Medusa's head: all the world's features harden, a deadly, ice-cold battle' is taken from the posthumous fragments of Nietzsche's writings in the winter of 1884–5.

The quotes on page 49 are taken from 'That Sleepless Flame' by Roberto Obregón (1940–), a Guatemalan poet, the author of five books, who was captured and disappeared somewhere along the Guatemala-El Salvador border in 1970. This translation was taken from *Volcán*, edited by Alejandro Murguía and Barbara Paschke, City Lights Books (1983).

Excerpt on page 55 from 'Regeneration' by Henry Vaughan (1621–95) from *Silex Scintillans* (1651).

'The heart turns to a stone, but it endures,' on page 62 is taken from 'Clair de Lune' by Anthony Hecht (1923–2004). *Collected Earlier Poems* by Anthony Hecht, Oxford University Press (1991).

Excerpt from 'I'm Going to Plant a Heart on the Earth' on page 65 by Rosario Murillo (1950–). This translation was taken from *Volcán*, edited by Alejandro Murguía and Barbara Paschke, City Lights Books (1983).

The author gratefully acknowledges the inspiration offered to her from the fragments of these writers' work.

Galatea

Then fell the word of stone on
My still existing, still heaving breast.
Never mind, I was not unprepared, and
Shall manage to adjust to it somehow.

Thank God, I've many things to do today—I
Need to kill and kill again
My memory, turn my heart to stone.

ANNA AKHMATOVA

We felt
A stone heart quicken, a deep fault made whole.

JAMES MERRILL

The Service of the Heart

A mirror-fragment snares blood-hues
From the cavern as if the dreamings
Of heart run on—whether by sequel or piety,
Something vexed and exquisitely
Ruined works its cure.

The hands of others excite each breastbone
To its crux, winging the world through the vessel.
Red admiral of heart-muscle—
A figment in the passage, its tidings dammed,
Each wave weaned from an ocean
Broken of habit.

Arbitrary heart, seized to a beleaguered fist,
Pendent in depth's darkness, uninvited, blood-
      guilty.
Alarmed by its discord, it rattles the balusters,
Disclosing its whereabouts to the spectres
Of prehistory, thrilling the weir like sturgeon,
Stirring and baiting it, stirring and engulfing.

I recall the astral light of the snow
And the deadening of rapture as he
Said to me, *You must go,*
How every volte in his withdrawal
Confessed to barbaric renewal.

He was a god disbelieving his own ability
To be extinguished; anointed by the wounds
Of her kisses, he said, *I cannot die,*
Blood from his mouth like briar-roses
Each with their own tiny voice,
He tried to silence them but the roses
Found their tongues, *Oh Kay,* they said,
We have been in the earth where
The dead are.

Now, the corpse of light converses from its
        graveyard
Of unmade bedclothes, culvert, clenched fist,
Teasing the mirage of daylight from the menisci
Of snowflakes — as if the looking-glass of the sky
Ruins itself to bathe us in a thousand fragments
Of the world-soul.

In the glory of limitless reflection, he gazes
Through a fraction of her caste
At the hilt of his beating mind; there it lies
In the dark like a trap in the heart-
Wood, reconstituting by memory the cold regent of the sky
To a Hall of Mirrors, where, by a single shard
His image builds itself infinitely
To the insatiate small shards of him, cut by a vanity
That is itself and reins itself with pitiless patience.

In 1901, an experiment was conducted
by Raymond Dodge and Thomas Cline
to plot the motion of a person's gaze
by attaching the flake of a mirror
to the cornea.

Immanent as sea to the shell intones,
Histories sounding once bred in the bone.

'Sleeping Beauty with Floating Roses', 1910,
from a collection of memorial photographs.

What delights me is the part of me to become this girl —
Her outline an iceberg in the death-world,
Persevering fragilely like memories of passion.
Who wonders what she might have let slip to devour
Of the world's prospects? Bare possibility weighed down
By the logic of rotten fruit upon the garden floor.

Now, the ultraviolet womb is sunk beneath her,
Closing ranks upon the grail of another,
And her body cherishes not the disco-purple of those lips
Like a gentle handbag's clasp—instead elapse
The same generous tulips of flesh, as if her body of chance
Had always envied what she thought of as ugly, the corpse
Delighting in the swallowing of her inheritance:

The Sodom of her bruised heart, atrophied fruit of Eden.
O that I might love my unbeautying.

I

The right arm was bent in against the chest,
as if defensively. She lay on her back, her head twisted
to one side, her left arm outstretched, a blindfold across her eyes.
A stone ballasted her body.

Truth finds its overtures in a stranger's hands,
The body's faulted braille resounds
      in decadence
Across all surfaces, the dreamings of stretchmarks
Suggest the body overawed by hours, *s-t-r-e-t-c-h*,
As we are overawed when the first hands wring
As if holding pomanders, bruising orange
To release the perfume, *commendatio animae*,
Commendation of soul to deity.

Strangeness comes to us all at the limits of Eros,
Where tenderness, by the gradual
      erosion
Of each small act of worship, mercerises the flesh
Of the love-feast, rendering the body revelational.

II

The hair, reddish-gold from the effects of the bog acids
in Schleswig-Holstein, was of exceptional fineness.
She had been led to the moor naked and drowned
in twenty inches of water.

The skull has been forsaken—
        Dug up like a gold nugget
A good fist of sun,
        Flagrant and rugged
As a staled brassiere-cup—
        The voice curled and stillborn.

Touch it with your fingertip:
        Its tenants efface all committals
Set in twenty-four carat bone,
        Extinguishing the helical
Flame of stubborn hair like afterbirth.
        All is erased. All forgotten.

When hostility to worth
        By nightjar and mere prevails,
Raindrops fall to earth
        As dead as bitten nails,
Casual forelocks of lifetime deposited
        Into winter's degrees of depth.

Polar. Unvisited.
    Upon the wealthy skull, a million
Shadows hourly deface.
    But this stickleback bullion
Speaks beyond the flag's apex.
        There remains a vestigial face,
        A sweetheart's derelict complex.

III

A man's body lay sixteen feet
to the side of her, anchored by branches.

For she breathes still, cast
        By clods and stones.
Her inviolate face remains,
        Flesh as white and hard as pearmain.
Echoes make uneasy moans
        Of her deliverance prayers, those who crest
Her prairie-grave have strict hearts
        Unfit to listen.
Is there nobody among these multitudes
        To summon her from the coals-
Bed? For flesh is born to sorrow,

As is written in intervening seams: the rules
        That govern all feuds
Of women to woman, and women unto men.

IV

mearc-stapas 'prowling the moors, huge
marauders / from some other world.'

I am the conquest of philandering night!
The widow of daylight.

Unwomaned, ungodded, unbegotten —
My dark kist of flesh treads on,

Stalking the bolt in the stone
Where what might have conjured into light

Gives up its voice, absolving to the night air
One flawless note like a spear.

V

Up ewich ungedeelt
   Forever undivided

All that lives, or can be, comes
In the act of tendering its resignation
      from the world;
The nascent grasstops, the nascent poems
Slayed by the tenets of devotion.

As the sun recites its nuptials of purgatory,
Rudiments, like thieves, transform into idols
      by common instinct
And by resignation to the fatal oar of the instant,
Petals become offertory.

Where the flames of grasstops bequeath
Their gentle ovations to the fates,
A kind of word-magic hauls the inmost hour,
      in the German tongue,

sprachgefühl, to the authorship of death.

Schleswig and Holstein belonged
to both Germany and Denmark at different times,
or else were independent.

Only the dead can be forgiven; But when I
Think of that my tongue's a stone.

What is there that might gate our
    derangement?
The heart's sorrow, *lacrimae rerum*, in each deathly hour.
The dead and all that is left unsaid cloistered by
    the atriums,
Each throb agitating the stone-strangury
    of our faces.

The belfry of the ribcage announces
Its delirium first by grace, soon by dissonance,
All its intimate tragedies releasing chance
From the stranglehold of passion's umbilicus,
Leashed to the breast, to absoluteness,
Upon which the intended measure pounces.

We are told we must worship the body,
In which the deeds of our time
Become veiled by the limiting powers
    of memory,
But only rarely, in the tenderest hours,

Do the tongues of the vanished chime
In our inmost sanctuary.

The Greek poet-philosopher, Nikos Kazantzakis corresponded with his first wife, Galatea, who resided in Athens, from his various journeys through Austria, Germany, and Italy from 1920-4. In her letters, Galatea conveys to Nikos the political and intellectual climate in Athens, a source of continual disappointment to him. He does not return home to her.

The body is the sarcophagus for one passion
While remaining the relic for another,
As if, among the world's lovers, one must
Always perform the role of sacramentalist, whose feast-
Day admits the sinew of infidelity that steers hands
  to worship another.

    The world is divided in two—good and bad,
    Above and below, God and anti-God.

Throughout the affair, their hands' stigmata confessed
All those buried inconsistencies of fascination,
The great unspoken truth that pandemonium
Touches off the stubborn bottom
  of our hearts.
The words, 'I adore', *o auorer*, the prayer of rebirth—
Emotion inaugurated by the death
  of prior love.

Terrifying news from Greece is reaching us here.
Will the wretched Greeks come to their senses now?
Will this catastrophe be the beginning of a new rebirth?

How like old countries the lovers were: misshaped
By a thousand histories, a source of nostalgia to few,
Unvisited by countless others. But more than this — they knew
To evolve beyond themselves, beyond their inheritance,
Beyond the schemes of recognition. They escaped
To roam an abundance of shadows, and adored
And abandoned the adored without penance.

When I talk about these matters, my belly is on fire,
I think in leaps, I take many unknown things as known,
I am on fire.

Perhaps the unknown god is the adulterer —
All his wants unpacked by the dressing-room door.
For love is a kind of patriotism, bed-fellow
Of disillusionment, as our homeland
Becomes under scrutiny inexistent,
So the territory of the beloved or the beguiling
Swiftly becomes the object of exiling, a source
Of stifling ennui from which we yearn to break free.

Magdalene jumped up and paced back and forth

Between the fire and the door. Her mind had grown furious.
A whirlwind had arisen and the pomegranates in the garden
Knocked against one another and were ready to break.

Everything visible is connected to the invisible.

Beyond all wounds with their memorial
Of kisses lie things unrealised as unrealisable,
The miraculous distance of incompleteness, as if all
    sensations announce
Our experience at the boundary of terrible heavens.

The weight of attachment seems suspended
At the lychgate of the rend, where lamed
Inclinations associate with shadow.
Somewhere, clandestinely, the ghost of the limb
    continues its actions
As if empty air were a transubstantiation of passion.

Or as we imagine terror erupts from a grey
And diffident sea of infinites like the mien
    of a dreaded friend,
Since the terror has been forever standing by,
Tantalised by the good reign coming.

Dead flies turn the perfumer's ointment fetid and putrid;
so a little folly outweighs massive wisdom.

Flies are on their backs on the timber window-
Sills, legs slowly careening as if death is a dance astern.

The drone is the sighs when I make love, as if someone
Might misinterpret each orgasm as a deathblow.

So I sweep up the dying flies and cast before swine
Their grating passions, raptures to irretraceable flight.

Only they're still there, careening through my mind
And into this poem. And when I come tonight,

I will know that the flies are dying inside the bin
Downstairs, asking me to sound the affinities.

    A kind of god will whistle to the flies at the ends
    Of the oblationary shaft that is the throat
       of an angel.
    None shall hinder the sullen flies' obedience,
    Their mindless dirge summons night to the mercy-seat.

And the eyes of the stone-blind shall see
Even in darkness and sophistry.

What I smelled first was her lover's spunk—
frankincense of someone else's life.

I wiggled my fingers into the finger-spaces of wool,
my cuckoo-hand inside more than just her glove,

thrust inside the grotto of her womb,
the swart pips of my atoms reincarnated within her.

I was born of her, I saw her life. My hand within her glove
as if I was her child, I saw her life—a ghostly cheiromancer,

whose tools of intuition graze against the omens
of desirelessness, the embalmed terrors of indifference

that yet shall spell out their merciless *sang froid*,
animating the brutal clinch.

For I have slain a man to my wounding, and a young man to my hurt.

In the modern world, let us not displease lovely touch.
Lamech and Zillah possessed such instinct once.
Now we announce by palm and thumb's trace
    the world's semantics,
All prospects for recognition held in abeyance
As the blizzard of touch brings dissimilar geometries
To monotony. In the oblivion of a miscarried embrace,
We submit our judgement to others; our fingertips
Neither grant independence nor cherish eclipse.

O let us not displease lovely touch.
On such a day, the small gods of heart's-ease
Will jettison the long measure of our lives,
Scene by scene, stroke by stroke, their titillations
Against the frigid cataracts of our veins.

Some Lot's wife
looking back
slowly turns to stone.

The grasp in life is desiring,
Desire hitched to our eyes like fish-hooks,
Master of their focus. How I
Look to stow beyond this universe of singular desire.

I want to look into the naked God,
And tell you what I felt.
Not the dead-eyes of words words   words—
Only that which inaugurates a fault
In your bound, unquestioned body.

My love, don't make of our marriage a blindfold—
Organs of tenderness out in the cold,
The season of kith belied
By the season of kist, unsought world.
Hoodwinked, without woman you fall uneyed,
Unsexed, the purple bracts and bold

Flower-heads of Jerusalem's artichoke
Submit to the unheard ruin of earth.

For all the imperfections wrought by womans-work
Upon my body, I would have you judge its worth
By your swollen cock.
                              "Turn back
and look at me, Lot. Look at your wife. The path
Goes on without you. Wreck
That which seeks to be mastered
While the degrees of attraction are ruled
By the degrees of absence preceding—"

"—wait. I see something.

The departed glory of our city!

              O pity!

The unsighted tread a measure,

Their arms outstretched as if they waltz

With an imaginary lover.

They stray blindly through the streets,

Spoiled by blood, their eyes pining away

In vain for delivery . . .

. . . I see something else. You. Your face

At the mercy of light.

O G–d, O G–d, O G–d. Refuse—"

The practice of *Sati* sees the widow
burn herself upon her husband's funeral pyre.

The scolding angel clarifies the uncertain
Boundaries of her body as she treads the coals, fire

Fanning from the crowning sparks of her hair. The damascene
Carvings of flames herald an original warfare.

Stare at her! The anatomised woman,
Perfected by her intimate holocaust.

Her nakedness does not debase or summon.
Her tiny singed breasts are flung down. Defused.

One affinity dawns, another the night betrays,
But the earth shares nobody's blood, and stays.

The Witch cried:

> *King of England thou shalt not be.*
> *Rise up stick, and stand still stone,*
> *For King of England thou shalt none.*

At the cardinal point, the flesh showed signs
Of becoming hard-grained —
Outflowing affections encountered air, leavening
First to burls, later to gargoyles. When
Witching established in sinew and bone
Assize and tyranny in equal measure, then
She was made triumphant and he, the King Stone.

Confronting is like descending into the waters of the Nile

I wear the waves like the world's grave-clothes,
The night-sky and all her memory of stars
Caught in the drag-net of my passage.
I am up to my knees. I am up to my thighs.

These sympathies of stone began in my heart
Until my heart was shingled and sank the depths
Of my body like a dying devilfish,
Dewlap of gills snagging on eddies, suggesting

The last life in the heart, and the first doomed life
In the petals of the Rose of Jericho,
(The word's echo like a sonar pulse
In the fluids of my chest, in the waters of the Nile).

I am up to my waist. I am up to my breasts.
My stone heart fixes attitudes in its stone of emptiness.
Some heat remains in the kiln's core
To heave a few small promises to the surface,

Where, wave-berthed, they cry out
As admiring stones cry out from the voices
Embedded in their spirituous meat.
I am up to my throat. I am up to my lips.

and coming face to face with

Now the minor tongues of the waters enter me,
Surrendered from such bodies, the river's dew.
On the riverbed, all truths are impressions,
The boulders and I are the only absolutes.

I am up to my brow. I am up to my crown.
My entry-ways are faults with obstinate memories.

something huge and cold and grey
that may once have been born of woman
but with the passing of ages has retreated into stone.

Follow
Into utterness,
Into dizzying chaos,—
The eternal boiling chaos
Of my locks!

Behold thy lover,—
Stone!

Overnight the squirrel turned
To stone, wintered to kilned-
    clay.
The careless pistons of venomous hair
Instantly dulled its body to slate,
Its hands reinforced to prayer.

Moles in foul cloisters missed its counterweight,
And surfaced towards the pith
Of its death like clots driving to the heart,
Their pilgrimage skulled by the tarmac path.
Yet children on the road's flank
Dreamed of entering the squirrel's mouth, still grilse-pink.
They stared and stared and stared
Until something in them declared
Consonance with it, their blood
Knitted to the squirrel's monkish hood.
From the Gorgon's world came this slogan—

Look at me! Look at me!
I will make you love me.
La belle indifférence wrings wits to stone.

I

In sculpture exercis'd his happy skill,
And carv'd in iv'ry such a maid; so fair
As Nature could not with his art compare,
Were she to work.

Pacific are my hands tonight, the minds
Drumming in their roadless tips, limed
As if they had, an hour before, daubed day to night,
Carrying off the taint of the deathly light,
Or as memory ghosts at the close
Of activity, the burning loss
Of her inner thigh
Still acting upon my fingers. Why
Can the charge of flesh not give the lie to immunity,
Its chasteness of gypsum; plaster saint—she,
Whose striae of blood-envy and the planchette
Of her sternum inscribe the working habits
Of how I—and men as me—notion
To sleep, lovelock and ambition.

II

His hand on her hard bosom lay: hard it was, beginning to relent,
It seem'd, the breast beneath his fingers bent;
He felt again, his fingers made a print;
'Twas flesh, but flesh so firm, it rose against the dint.

He yearns for accomplishment, and vests
With this yearning each carving of the purple
Crocus. He designs me to the scales of infinity,
A perfect plane of tesselation, each cell of marble
Nests infinitesimal versions of me   of me
        of me.

Enamoured of knowledge, blood sings in its rich
        maze,
Of the encrypted heiroglyphs that detail
All motions to death, attesting to the fire
Locked in clear and clarion hearts. Sire,
No single touch can be the reciprocal
Of your fingers. Of those full fathoms of flesh,
You must submit to casket and ruin
All this quarried consummation.

The Battle of Jutland, between Britain and Germany, was
the largest naval battle of the First World War in the
North Sea near Denmark. The first shots were fired from
the British ship, HMS Galatea. The British lost 14 ships
and 6094 men. The Germans lost 11 ships and 2551 men.
Both sides claimed victory.

The Spark of Transgression

I

Danae was seduced by Zeus,
who penetrated her bronze cell in a shower of gold.

It began by the gentleness of gold
And ended in the prolific hold
Of her stern governance. Posterity and brutish
Innocence working into the blush
Of her lips, melting her tanned breastplate
Into the tenderness of his pallet.

All hard edges perished from the earth
Vitrifying into the rivers of her desire—
His father's radical traits inherited by birth.
Blood-lustred at her side, he wore
The scarlet helmet of his caul
And the rictus of an ancestral quarrel.

II

Finding his daughter withchild, Acrisius shut her
and her newborn child into a chest
and cast them into the sea.

Naked, you harked back to my father in the bath, his genitalia
rippling in the water like a purple emperor.
I tweaked a nipple, *Sorry won't touch it again,*
that harked back to my foetal body, arcane
as a paper-germ dreaming of pages, caressed
by the promise of fingers. And back to the blackness,
rife and immanent, upon whose surface
echoes of the Holy Ghost assembled your vanished embrace.

You cannot guess, O my son,
The griefs that disease this heart of mine;
You spend your dreams against my breast,
Unaroused by the confines of our chest
Or the water's infatuation—
By the dead reckoning of its whims, we near our destination.

Shall our hands ever touch the resurrecting corpus
of this elapsed sea
Or by our sides be quiet as to the hands of statues
That no kisses might inherit their abandoned fires?

III

Perseus himself, the son of Danae, was at full stretch,
like one who hurries and shudders with horror.
After him rushed the Gorgons, unapproachable and unspeakable,
longing to seize him . . . their tongues flickering, and their teeth gnashing
with fury, and their eyes glaring fiercely. And upon the awful heads
of the Gorgons great fear was quaking.

Each word in the ear wings my soles to vagrancy.
Leave me to the habits of the sophist.
The space behind me quills as if the air was kissed
By your hungry mouth, and stirred to urgency.

Do not ask me to turn, mother!

Let the grasstops be worthy, let them have a claim
On my birthright. Are my traits not heritable
By sod and turf as by the bloodlines of the ardent stable?
Croon the assault of my cradle to the grass that I wist not such shame.

IV

The Gorgon's face has been used by many cultures in doorways
and on shields to turn away evil by its own horrors to prevent or avert war.

Great thought is like Medusa's head:
all the world's features harden, a deadly, ice-cold battle.

Gone is the custom of keeping another in mind:
Such an act petrifies, our measures halted to another's needs.
The delirium of our lives chased to the cardinal points,
Where the blitz fires flesh to insensibility.
Only in the fury of the loins' errands,
And by the plaint of our hearts,
And upon the faults of earlier generations—

Craft it from ordure and scalplock
And with the phlegm of a stung heart.
Rivet its teeth by an edge.
Widen its sights by electric shock.
The earthing of the mask upon our front parts:
The congress of causal and carnage.

For love is fierce as death, passion is mighty as Sheol;
Its darts are darts of fire, a blazing flame.

People of the city take air and modesty unclad,
Careful not to rouse in flesh and blood
Gestures hibernating in schist —
Their skulls become an almshouse,
Their mouths stooped where kissed.

Every play of feature is a rebuttal
Weighed against itself. And even their speech
Relies upon the most extraordinary juggle
    of substance.
The folk are reigned by rigor
And calculation. None shall breach
The keep, and no sense shall transfigure.

∽

And yet inside each one. The fire appears to be boundless.
Its analogues flatter every surface like Brocken flames
Upon the grey cuirass of mountains, mocking, intoxicating.
The fire-ship anchors in the pit of the stomach,
Spits hackbut, howitzer and snickersnee. If you should reach
Inside, your calluses would sting immediately
And the stealth of flames would lap your hand to the bracelet
Of its wrist, leaving behind the soft endeavour of a handshake—
Fleshing what was hardened, threshing sympathies to the break.

Men who have loved much,
or who have never been on the brink of a woman.

It is a heart that he throws down, sowing
Its incendiary secrets into other lives.

The shrapnel of unrecognised affinity
Scathing the surface of tact.

How the unannounced radiance
Of rapture

Long years into impotence
Kindled his obsessions —

The forgotten élan
Of a once virile man.

They say he is burdened in his afterlife
with scalding stones.

For a fire has shed lustre in my ego,
It blazes against you.

Impacted gold of the perished and the unborn,
Wayfaring the globe of the body like tiny suns.

Every hour the body sheds or raises some old affinity—
The universe's desires for life and death cached inside us, *humus*;
    gone to earth.

Reinstate to the hollow air those that are lamented
In all quarters of the body, O globe,

The heart is in anguish. The heart suffers,
Weighted down with ciphers

And with shyness. The globe has become
    a thing unclean,
As life absolves itself in the bosom.

Exclaim its possessions to the hollow night.
Discharge your heart like nectar-wine
Into the unrelieved darkness.

And begin again.

He desired her. The verboten atom of lust
Seared his loins like the spark of instinct or Eos
Spreading a seam of gold to the core of him
Bringing him to the fruition of his humanity—
No more did he feel like a god dighted and deified
By the rigging of his masculinity.

And the infernal machine of lust detonated
Its Greek Fire among the silt and sediment of his body,
Stirring the causes of propagation and plenum,
The bloody causes with pyrite at their core,
Always at the ready. Always spoiling for.
He would make her cry. That would be his bent.

Her tears would pay his heart's annuity.

> As well as certain women who were healed
> of evil spirits, Mary, who was called Magdalene,
> from whom seven demons had gone out.
> He ministered them out of their possessions.

In the dark of the museum's unhallowed arcs,
They have hitched high the lazuli coma of her fin,
Lashing the bearded pannier of her craw.
Mortified, bellying the air—Ocean Boudicca—
Gliding as a jumbo-jet, the ocean her night-terror.

The philosophic smile brooks all agonies,
    willing sacrifice,
And the afterthought eye, like a portrait's intimate study,
Plays shadows from the mind's den—
For an apocalypse of all that is undergone,
Unctiously, earnestly, flesh the decoy.

Her gargantuan heart is the holy ark, a fleshy jeroboam
Whose brew is the *Weltliebe* wherein the infinite
Possibilities of human love find glittering passage;
Or a subsidiary brain in whose glistening sanctum
Man's *Sturm und Drang* silts like tealeaves in porcelain.

Subdued to so much meat, she's heavy
In the air, drowning beneath her fathoms,
The mighty eloquence of her breast-stroke, attuned
To the echoes of waves, leadens to extinction,
Blood's alchemy conjuring the glorious jeroboam
    into a tomb.

Everyman has recurring dreams in which he swims
Through her veins, intending to his profoundest depths,
Sifting for perfection as her magnitude commands.
In the dark, all eyes askance, the memories
Of her monolithic ego begin to heave.

                    Only a little Fountain lent
                              Some use for Eares,
          And on the dumbe shades language spent
                    The musick of her teares;
                    I drew her neare, and found
                              The Cisterne full
          Of divers stones, some bright, and round
                    Others ill-shap'd, and dull.

Afterwards we ate a bowl of peas
full of hidden voices,
their tiny green backs curled like ferns.
I gazed at it—ceramic pool
of divers stones   holy
I saw one minute ovum   perfect
and the colour of wetted grass, wend slowly slowly
through the canal of my oesophagus,
determining the tracts of lung gut sphincter,
me birthing it whole, sparkling green,
a snakes-egg.
          There is unknown desire
in these smallest and least understood
artifacts—*divers stones* whose ounces
of rigorous flesh inhere
memories of frontcrawling beyond
the gently-applauding fimbria, beyond
the penitent outflow of ocean
whence, the detonation of all
that is incarnational.

Our words were as dew-fall upon Damascus;
As for the dusk rain, they desired us.

I have a fantasy in which I am dead,
the garnet-wattle of my skin
harmonising with the garnet I inherited
from my grandmother
as if I am transforming into this garnet, flesh
to painted marble to flesh-gem,
as if I was never alive.

I am busy with the sorcery of bone-
becoming, retrenching skin
and muscle rake my lips apart,
violet mouth opening,
opening the way the prodigal wings
of oceans hie anxiously from each other,
or as if my spirit is huge: glowing neck
of a songbird extending to give birth
to me, to my soul.

But I am not soul in my fantasy,
I am the dead, I am become a tree,
ignored as trees are, I am that same
living and barky texture of death,
and the flesh-oaths of my nipples
are the dark-clay cancers of burls,
I am burlesque of living-me,
I am what Jesus risen must have been,
copper underlife of the body's triumph.

When I pass from the earth, the wake of the sun,
By sleight of gold,
Will surgeon the deadly heart and grant me an un-
    fledged
Heart, its angst wrung out in rageless blood.

        Behold!

In 2005, 500 naked people take to the streets
of America and England for artist, Spencer Tunick.
One woman gets her period.

Simply to worship the parade of soft eaves
Cannot grant the measures to familiarities,
Or even the guise of perspectives, being on the face
    of it only.
For what occurs intrinsically, of chitterling and cell,
Goes to the making of face, defining as weft to the tapestry.
Why then should the merest glimpse of the unravelled threads
Of the visceral being give occasion for dismay?

As if we are the derelict of ungentle invention
Come to the wilderness of sin
Swaddled in the dreads of Canaan
That in absconding blood comes imperfect knowledge—
Nighted by its veil, we hear the screams at Babi Yar
The scalding child on the road to Vietkong.
Here is the hecatomb from whence we were born
And in which we live on. The marred
Consequences of our love, the buried rage
    of our creator
Whose voice finds its passage by posies
Or by these mild and anticipated issues
Attainting us, "Dross begun, and dross
    you will become."

        Hence we abandon the authors of our existence,
        Tranced by figments of flesh stripped at our insistence.

Sprinkle on them waters of atonement; they have caused
A razor to pass over all their flesh.

Unguessed in the hotbed, awaiting discovery,
The ghost-lives of children breathing their intentions
Inside me like mist, I prayed for thee.
I prayed for thee, *O mother, accouche*
Accouche to consanguinity
Your daughter to the headwaters.

Imparting my sum and substance as a *fait accompli*
Upon the earthweight, laid open to the historicity
Of this hour, this life, how I prayed for thee.
How I begged for thee, *O mother, accouche*
Accouche your only daughter
To the atoning waters of our sorority.

It docked towards me, and snatched,
wrenching a jumbo steak of me
a whole verse of my body's poem
the *vers libre* that began, *let-me-touch*,
and finished, *don't-let-me-go*. Swallowed
early cinnabar crowns, Peters-pence,
took inside the forget-me-not-blue
of its mouth my whole arm
like baby-Moses returned to the amnion.
My whole arm, its kissed hub
of shoulder, unbirthed
inside this shark, circling, rose-grey
coelenterate of womb
floating in the sea's astonishing
fuselage, as if the sea is a woman.
I watched in the shark's spaceship-port-
hole-eye my arm like Venus gliding
past, into the vast Venice of outer-space,
as if this shark was a woman, or space
could be the body of a woman.
I felt the shark's hide coast over me
until I was this shark,
the erogenous deeps of the Pacific
welled in me such rapture, such glee:
the shark inside
inside this body that I am.

    And I am sublime.
    I will embody all ruined expanses.

The heart turns to a stone, but it endures.

My god—
    Let there always be this heat.
Let there be no death of feeling,
For if the heart is the sun, its defeat
Will defeat all things.

Transform the Hell that slurs upon
Our catchpenny machines; incarnate beyond
A Manichean engine, a fire-devourer
Flaunting pluck as valour.

Synchronise these hearts of our disgrace, taciturn
As a chain-gang; the world's hyle
Combusted from within like oil,
Deadlocked by undisguised expression.

                ~

When, still emerging, the vestal sunlight
Strikes, we shield our eyes and, by aversion,
Motion to the pocketwatches
That counsel the hours and the assaults
Of affection. In this frontier century,
Only the soundings of the heart's blood
Keep the mysteries of their infinitudes,
Dropping away towards the eye
Of an unknown god.
    A scarce kind of music corrals us
Onwards to what we took for passion
But was, by the diminishing of returns,
Con-passio, sufferance,
The diminishing of our hearts to sepulchres.

And yet—
    Perhaps the many seeds of light
Shall germinate and turban down
The body of abandoned intrigues, spiring
The ages like Rapunzel's hair,
                  Aureate,
                        Annihilating death.

And the heart's grave is corrupted and kissed
By the hungry grass, which swallows to persist.

I'm going to leave a heart in the earth
So it may grow and flower.

Leave your heart in the earth
Its gracious mandrake nature
Gives heirs to the rhapsodies of our reign.
Slender shoots stir the senseless mire,
      disturbing embedded caresses,
From whose overcast materials comes the rebirth

Of all that we have adored, all that we have dared
To pour scorn on, all that we have brushed aside.
The atomic rendering of a generation's obsessions—
The clay of the goylem. Liebniz's monads.
The beautiful imprimis, our lifeblood
In the bud. The earliest spark of our transgressions.

Leave your heart in the earth that it might bloom
To the body's thwarted openness,
Gospels unspoken in life expressing their feverishness
In the fraught whispering of leaves at the close
Of their affiliations. Attend to the hymn
Of life's cowardice cadenced in all that grows.

Leave your heart in the night soil that the land
Of its birth, forgiving its presence, might bless the roots'
Passage through the seams of man and beast
To the seat of the globe's mercy.   And beyond.
To a new aurora by whose kindlier radiance the fruits
Of our arrested affections swell to their feast.